The Far

by

Illustrated by Sean O'Neill

PEARSON

Scott
Foresman

Editorial Offices: Glenview, Illinois • Parsippany, New Jersey • New York, New York
Sales Offices: Needham, Massachusetts • Duluth, Georgia • Glenview, Illinois
Coppell, Texas • Sacramento, California • Mesa, Arizona

The farmer went to feed the pig.
A big wind came along.
The wind blew the farmer's hat.
The farmer chased his hat.
The pig had to wait.

The farmer went to feed the cows.
The farmer's hat blew away.
The farmer chased his hat.
The cow had to wait.

hens

The farmer went to feed the hens.
The farmer's hat blew away.
The farmer chased his hat.
The hens had to wait.

The farmer went to feed the horses.
Soon the farmer chased his hat again.
"We never get our food fast!" said
the light brown horse.
"We always have to wait!"

The animals got together.
"We don't want to wait!" said the dark
brown horse.
"But the farmer's hat blows away," said
the big cow.
"He has to chase it."

"I can solve this problem," said
the spider.
"I will make something to fix the
farmer's hat."
The spider went to work spinning.

The spider made strings for the hat.
The farmer went to feed the animals.
His hat did not blow away!
They all said, "Thank you, spider!
Now we will not have to wait!"

8